WILL
ISIS
CAUSE
A NUCLEAR
WAR?

An Examination of Recent Events
According to Bible Prophecy

By Russell Redden

Will ISIS Cause A Nuclear War?
An Examination of Recent Events According to Bible Prophecy

ISBN-13: 978-1500633028

ISBN-10: 150063302X

Also by Russell Redden

The Seventh Shmita: Countdown to the Second Coming (2014)

Genesis and Jubilees: The Parallel Edition (2013)

Rise of the Assyrian: The Antichrist, the Beast, and the Revived Babylonian Empire
First Edition: 2006
Second Edition: 2008
Third Edition: 2012

Beyond Coincidence: The Testimony of Prophecy (2011)

WILL ISIS CAUSE A NUCLEAR WAR?

An Examination of Recent Events According to Bible Prophecy

By Russell Redden

Sections

INTRODUCTION

Several events have now occurred, which need to be addressed, in a quickly, and timely manner. After the pullout of U.S. troops in Iraq, the terrorists are taking over. These terrorists share an objective that will eventually occur, according to the prophecy of Psalm 83. This prophecy describes a coalition formed against Israel, which the Islamic State of Iraq (or ISIS)—now called the Islamic State of Iraq and the Levant (ISIL)—could easily fulfill.

ISIS could assemble the same players of the Psalm 83 coalition. Furthermore, it appears that Israel's ground invasion into Gaza could also be a catalyst for the assembly of these troops. The Gaza assault now inflaming the Arab world, and we are witnessing protests against Israel in the streets of London, and France.

While all of this upheaval has been going on, the Russian bear is on the move, taking military action against Ukraine. This nation borders the Black Sea, where phase II of the missile defense shield will be implemented. Russia has threatened to bomb these targets, if President Obama and N.A.T.O continue their plan for missile defense.

The potential for chaos on a Biblical scale is enormous; possibly greater than I have witnessed in my lifetime. However, the majority of people—including church—have fallen asleep to these dangers. The media does not focus on issues that make their President look bad. Therefore, news about these issues must be gathered from the Internet, not "mainstream" news sources, such as radio or television.

The United States trained ISIS, in an attempt to topple the president of Syria. This adds further suspicion in the eyes of Vladimir Putin, and other communists in Russia. They may fear—with or without just cause—that the United States has be infiltrated by a "Manchurian Candidate," with terrorist ties. This fear has been escalated by the fact that Barack Obama's half brother has also been accused of terrorism.

The expectation of some of these events are found in my 2006 book, *Rise of the Assyrian: the Antichrist, the Beast, and the Revived Babylonian Empire*. Syria, Jordan, and Lebanon are expected to fall. A call was expected for a coalition to be formed against Israel, as the Cold War is revived. Tensions were expected to rise between Russia and the United States.

For this reason, I have included portions of two chapters of this book, to provide context. The *timing* of these events also fits the premise of my new book the Seventh Shmita. The same method of interpreting Daniel's "Seventy Sevens" prophecy points to the *next* Jewish Sabbatical year as the time these events could literally explode, causing the most disastrous time in human history.

Russell Redden

THE PSALM 83 COALITION

From the Book "Rise of the Assyrian"
First published 2006

The promised judgment of Edom is one of the final events that will occur before the beginning of the Great Tribulation. There is a connection between Edom's destruction, and a confederacy of Arabs that will seek to destroy the Jewish state. This attempted invasion was predicted in this Psalm written by Asaph:

"Keep not thou silence, O God: hold not thy peace, and be not still, O God. For, lo, thine enemies make a tumult: and they that hate thee have lifted up the head. They have taken crafty counsel against thy people, and consulted against thy hidden ones. They have said, Come, and let us cut them off from being a nation; that the name of Israel may be no more in remembrance. For they have consulted together with one consent: they are confederate against thee: The tabernacles of Edom, and the Ishmaelites; of Moab, and the Hagarenes; Gebal, and Ammon, and Amalek; the Philistines with the inhabitants of Tyre; Assur also is joined with them: they have holpen the children of Lot. Selah." (Psalm 83:1-8)

This confederacy will be comprised of the "Ishmaelites," and the "Hagarenes," which were the ancestors of all Arab peoples. Joining with them are men from these specific geographic locations:

- **EDOM**— A kingdom in south-western Jordan
- **MOAB**— In northwestern Jordan
- **GEBAL**— A coastal city in modern day Lebanon, or a site near ancient Edom
- **AMMON**— In Jordan
- **AMALEK**— In western Jordan
- **THE PHILISTINES**— the Gaza Strip
- **TYRE**— In Lebanon

The Psalmist may have singled out these locations because this assault against Israel will be launched from these lands, the largest numbers of troops will be assembled from these regions, or both.

Joining with this confederacy is "Assur." "Assur" was the capitol city of Assyria, and the name of their highest god. In the eyes of the Assyrians, this god was the protector of the Assyrian nation. This name in the Bible is equivalent to Assyria, which is in modern day Iraq.

The Psalmist used terminology that reveals that this is a volunteer army of the general populace, not a coalition of national entities. We read:

"the <u>tents</u> of Edom and the Ishmaelites, Moab and the Hagrites (etc)..." (Psalm 83:6, English Standard Version)

Take note, the Psalmist wrote that the "tents" of these nations would form this coalition. The "tent" was the habitation of the common man. This strongly suggests that this army will be comprised of individuals, not nations. It will be a volunteer army with one common goal: to destroy Israel. Certainly, terrorist organizations such as Hizballah, and HAMAS fit this description, because they are all composed of volunteers, not armies drafted by nation states. The coalition of Asaph's prophecy would likely be assembled from every terrorist group, every sect, and every tribe.

THE CHILDREN OF LOT

This confederacy will aid the children of Lot, and we are to "meditate upon this" (a Selah.) We read:

"Assur also is joined with them: they have holpen the children of Lot. Selah." (Psalm 83:8)

The word translated "holpen" comes from the Hebrew word zerowa` [זְרוֹעַ,] which means "arm," "strength" or "strong arm," as it is translated in the English Standard Version:

"Asshur also has joined them; they are the strong arm of the children of Lot. Selah" (Psalm 83:8, English Standard Version)

The children of Lot dwelt in Western Jordan (in Moab, and Ammon), near ancient Edom. The Psalmist wrote that Assur is united with this coalition to give assistance to these Jordanian Arabs.

Since this battle will occur in the future, the government of Jordan will likely fall into the hands of radical extremists. Of course, it is possible that there could be an uprising against Israel that the current Jordanian government simply will not be able to contain. Either scenario could occur today. Recently, Osama Bin Lauden suggested that Muslims cross the Jordanian border to launch a future attack against the Jewish State:

"Al-Qaida leader Osama bin Laden's latest audio message has targeted Jordan for the first time, calling on his supporters to infiltrate the country in order to "liberate al-Aksa," according to the Middle East Media Research Institute (MEMRI)." (From: BIN LADEN CALLS FOR INFILTRATION OF JORDAN AS WAY TO 'LIBERATE AL-AKSA', Jerusalem Post, March 17, 2009)

Jordan is presently a moderate government, which signed a peace treaty with Israel in 1994. However, the populace contains many radical extremists, who are supportive of Bin Laden, and the radical Islamic movement. The seeds of a future attack against Israel may have been sown by Bin Laden—but this prophecy will be fulfilled after the prince from Assyria assembles this coalition.

THE DESTRUCTION OF THESE TROOPS

This prophecy appears to describe a nuclear strike against this coalition of Arabs, for they will be disintegrated instantly by fire. In Psalm 83 verses 2-14, we read:

"Do unto them as unto the Midianites; as to Sisera, as to Jabin, at the brook of Kison: Which perished at Endor: they became as dung for the earth. Make their nobles like Oreb, and like Zeeb: yea, all their princes as Zebah, and as Zalmunna: Who said, Let us take to ourselves the houses of God in possession. <u>O my God, make them like a wheel; as the stubble before the wind. As the fire burneth a wood, and as the flame setteth the mountains on fire.</u> So persecute them with thy tempest, and make them afraid with thy storm. Fill their faces with shame; that they may seek thy name, O LORD. Let them be confounded and troubled for ever; yea, let them be put to shame, and perish: That men may know that thou, whose name alone is JEHOVAH, art the most high over all the earth." (Psalm 83:9-18)

This Psalm predicts that fire will instantly turn this coalition of Arab troops into *stubble*, that will be blown away by a "tempest" (or strong wind.) The word "stubble" in the Hebrew means, "chaff[1]." Nuclear weapons would cause a fire, a shattering wind, and would disintegrate people instantly—as predicted in this Psalm.

Since this confederacy gives aid to "the children of Lot," who dwelt in Western Jordan, this is obviously the location where this fire

---
[1] קַשׁ *qash*

will fall. This parallels a prophecy written by the prophet Isaiah. He described a great destruction coming upon the first nation listed in this prophecy—ancient Edom. As the Psalmist predicted fire would fall on this confederacy, Isaiah predicted that the land of Edom would become a burning pitch.

THE JUDGMENT OF EDOM

Edom was an empire located in southwestern Jordan, along the Israeli border, an obvious place to stage an attack against the Jewish state. The context of Isaiah's prophecy is the time when God's judgment will fall upon all nations. This parallels the book of Revelation, which quotes this prophecy, and specifies that this battle will occur as "the great day" of God's wrath falls on the earth. In Isaiah chapter 34, we read:

"Come near, ye nations, to hear; and hearken, ye people: let the earth hear, and all that is therein; the world, and all things that come forth of it. For the indignation of the LORD is upon all nations, and his fury upon all their armies: he hath utterly destroyed them, he hath delivered them to the slaughter. Their slain also shall be cast out, and their stink shall come up out of their carcases, and the mountains shall be melted with their blood. And all the host of heaven shall be dissolved, and the heavens shall be rolled together as a scroll: and all their host shall fall down, as the leaf falleth off from the vine, and as a falling fig from the fig tree. For my sword shall be bathed in heaven: behold, it shall come down upon Idumea, and upon the people of my curse, to judgment. The sword of the LORD is filled with blood, it is made fat with fatness, and with the blood of lambs and goats, with the fat of the kidneys of rams: for the LORD hath a sacrifice in Bozrah, and a great slaughter in the land of Idumea." (Isaiah 34:1-6)

This judgment will fall upon "Idumea," and also "the people of my curse[1]." Biblical dictionaries affirm that Idumea is another name for ancient Edom. The judgment of Edom will occur when "the indignation of the LORD is upon *all* nations," which is the Great Tribulation.

When Edom is laid waste, the heavens will "roll together as a scroll." The word translated "heavens" in the Hebrew can mean the "heaven" of God's domain, the "heaven" of the universe, or the "heaven" of the sky[2]. Since this judgment will fall on Edom, the sky is obviously the subject of Isaiah's prophecy.

Isaiah also predicted that the "host" (or stars) of heaven will "fall to the ground," and be "dissolved[3]." Obviously, since the stars of the universe cannot literally "fall to the ground" or be dissolved, this language must describe something similar.

If we compare Isaiah's prophecy to the effects of nuclear weapons, we find that they are one and the same. Atomic weapons create mushroom clouds. If exploded high in the air, the blast waves cause the sky to roll inward, and then outward. To ancient man, this mushroom cloud could appear as though the sky is being rolled like a scroll.

Atomic weapons reproduce the same nuclear fission that occurs within the sun. Small stars are temporarily created in this process. Therefore, the phrase "the stars fell from the heavens" is completely accurate. Furthermore, the soot, and smoke caused by the fires of these atomic weapons would cause the stars to disappear from the sky for a period of time. Isaiah also described the mountains being melted at the same time as the blood of men.

Since Isaiah's prophecy is a future event, and man possesses nuclear weapons, it is a logical conclusion that they will be used against these troops who gather in ancient Edom. It is known that Israel possesses nuclear weapons, even though this has not been officially declared. If threatened with their existence, the Jewish state

---

[1] After fire falls on Edom, fire will fall on one third of the earth—"the people of my [God's] curse."

[2] שָׁמַיִם shamayim

[3] מָקַק maqaq —"to decay"

would not hesitate to use them. For this reason, the army that will assemble in Jordan will likely be massive.

Isaiah continues to write that the "Judgment of Edom" will occur when there is a "controversy" over "Zion":

"For it is the day of the LORD'S vengeance, and the year of recompences for the controversy of Zion." (Isaiah 34:8)

"Zion" is another name for Jerusalem. The word "controversy" comes from a Hebrew word that means "quarrel" or "dispute[1]." The modern dispute over this city began in 1967, when the Israelis took it as a spoil of the Six Day War. Before this war, the Jews had not possessed this city since 70 A.D. Therefore, this "controversy" has only occurred during the past 50 years!

As we continue to read about Edom's Judgment, we find more evidence that nuclear weapons will be used to decimate this land:

"And the streams of Edom shall be turned into pitch, and her soil into sulfur; her land shall become burning pitch. Night and day it shall not be quenched; its smoke shall go up forever. From generation to generation it shall lie waste; none shall pass through it forever and ever." (Isaiah 34:9-10, English Standard Version)

The land of Edom will become a "burning pitch," and its streams will become "pitch." The word "pitch" comes from the Hebrew word *zepheth* [זֶפֶת.] This word describes a tar like-substance. Obviously, the water of these streams must be vaporized before being turned into "pitch." Additionally, Edom's dust will be "turned into sulfur."

These judgments of Edom describe a nuclear attack flawlessly. In the near future, Israel will be faced with a massive army assembled along its border, in the location of ancient Edom, and shall destroy these troops with fire.

---

[1] רִיב *riyb*

THE BOOK OF REVELATION

The Apostle John paraphrases Isaiah's prophecy of Edom's judgment, and declares that the Judgment Day of God begins with this event. In Revelation chapter 6, we read:

"And I beheld when he had opened the sixth seal, and, lo, there was a great earthquake; <u>and the sun became black as sackcloth of hair, and</u> <u>the moon became as blood; And the stars of heaven fell unto the earth,</u> <u>even as a fig tree casteth her untimely figs, when she is shaken of a</u> <u>mighty wind</u>. And <u>the heaven departed as a scroll when it is rolled</u> together; and every mountain and island were moved out of their places. And the kings of the earth, and the great men, and the rich men, and the chief captains, and the mighty men, and every bondman, and every free man, hid themselves in the dens and in the rocks of the mountains; And said to the mountains and rocks, Fall on us, and hide us from the face of him that sitteth on the throne, and from the wrath of the Lamb: <u>For the great day of his wrath is come; and who shall be able to stand?</u>" (Revelation 6:12-17)

John adds that "a great earthquake" will occur at the same time the "heavens depart as a scroll when it is rolled together." In the Greek, the word "departed" comes from a word that means, "to separate[1]." John wrote that the sky will roll *outward* as a scroll, and Isaiah wrote that it would roll *inward* as a scroll. Of course, the blast waves of atomic weapons do both. It is theorized that nuclear explosions could even have an impact upon fault lines—causing earthquakes, landslides, and tidal waves.

John quoted Isaiah when he wrote that the stars would fall from the sky. Isaiah also predicted these *stars* would disappear; John described the *sun* being darkened. Naturally, the same soot, and smoke that would blot out the stars would also block sunlight from reaching the earth for a period of time.

---
[1] ἀποχωρίζω *apochorizo*

John also wrote that when this disaster occurs, the men of the earth would hide underground, and declare that the great day of God's wrath has begun. They obviously are expecting some eminent disaster. As we will learn, one half hour after Edom's destruction, fire will destroy one third of the earth (Revelation 8:7.) After the nuclear missiles are launched, people would hide underground in fallout shelters, as these people hide underground.

The judgment of Edom will usher in the Judgment Day of God. The Arab confederacy assembled by Assur is obviously the catalyst for Edom's destruction. After fire falls upon this confederacy in western Jordan, it will fall on one third of the world.

EDOM DESTROYED AS SODOM AND GOMORRAH

Jeremiah predicted that Edom would be destroyed in the same manner as Sodom, and Gomorrah. Of course, these cities were destroyed with fire, and brimstone:

"Then the LORD rained upon Sodom and upon Gomorrah brimstone and fire from the LORD out of heaven; And he overthrew those cities, and all the plain, and all the inhabitants of the cities, and that which grew upon the ground. But his wife looked back from behind him, and she became a pillar of salt." (Genesis 19:24-26)

In the book of Jeremiah, we read:

"Also Edom shall be a desolation: every one that goeth by it shall be astonished, and shall hiss at all the plagues thereof. As in the overthrow of Sodom and Gomorrah and the neighbour cities thereof, saith the LORD, no man shall abide there, neither shall a son of man dwell in it. Behold, he shall come up like a lion from the swelling of Jordan against the habitation of the strong: but I will suddenly make him run away from her: and who is a chosen man, that I may appoint over her? for who is like me? and who will appoint me the time? and who is that shepherd that will stand before me? <u>Therefore hear the counsel of the</u> LORD, <u>that he hath taken against Edom; and his purposes, that he hath purposed against the inhabitants of Teman: Surely the least of the flock shall draw them out: surely he shall make their habitations desolate with them</u>. <u>The earth is moved at the noise of their fall</u>, at the cry the noise thereof was heard in the Red sea. Behold, he shall come up and fly as the eagle, and spread his wings over Bozrah: and at that day shall the heart of the mighty men of Edom be as the heart of a woman in her pangs." (Jeremiah 49:17-22)

Jeremiah predicted that the "least of the flock" will draw Edom out, and they will come against "the habitation of the strong," which is obviously Israel. In another passage, the prophet used the term, "least of the flock" for the king of Babylon:

"Therefore hear ye the counsel of the LORD, that he hath taken against Babylon; and his purposes, that he hath purposed against the land of the Chaldeans: Surely <u>the least of the flock shall draw them out</u>: surely he shall make their habitation desolate with them. At the noise of the taking of Babylon the earth is moved, and the cry is heard among the nations." (Jeremiah 50:45-46)

The same person responsible for Babylon's destruction at the end of the Great Tribulation will also cause Edom's destruction. He is the king of Babylon, the "least of the flock," the Assyrian who will be defeated by God when He returns. Jeremiah called the king of Babylon "the least of the flock" in a derogatory manner, and tied Edom's destruction to this ruler.

We also read, "The earth is moved at the noise of their fall, at the cry the noise thereof was heard in the Red Sea" (Jeremiah 49:21). The destruction coming upon the land once known as Edom will be massive, witnessed by the entire world.

EZEKIEL'S PREDICTION

Ezekiel prophesied that Edom would become desolate by the hands of the Jewish people. Therefore, they will obviously be responsible for its destruction by fire. We read in Ezekiel:

"Thus saith the Lord GOD; <u>Because that Edom hath dealt against the</u> <u>house of Judah by taking vengeance</u>, and hath greatly offended, and revenged himself upon them; Therefore thus saith the Lord GOD; I will also stretch out mine hand upon Edom, and will cut off man and Beast from it; and I will make it desolate from Teman; and they of Dedan shall fall by the sword. And <u>I will lay my vengeance upon Edom by the</u> <u>hand</u> of my people Israel: and they shall do in Edom according to mine anger and according to my fury; and they shall know my vengeance, saith the Lord GOD." (Ezekiel 25:12-14)

Edom will join with Assur in this confederacy, seeking to destroy Israel. As these troops gather in Jordan, God will use his people to destroy Edom, as promised. Of course, the "prince" of Assyria will dwell safely in his own land when this destruction occurs.

THE COVENANT

In the prophecy of Psalm 83, we read that a *confederacy* will be formed with Assur. In this passage, the word "confederate" comes from the word, *beriyth* [בְּרִית,] which means "a covenant." We literally read:

"For they conspire with one accord; against you they make a covenant [בְּרִית *beriyth*]—" (Psalm 83, English Standard Version)

In the book of Daniel, *this same* Hebrew word is used for the covenant made by the Little Horn. In Daniel chapter 9, we read:

"And he shall <u>confirm</u> the <u>covenant</u> [בְּרִית *beriyth*] with many for one week: and in the midst of the week he shall cause the sacrifice and the oblation to cease, and for the overspreading of abominations he shall make it desolate, even until the consummation, and that determined shall be poured upon the desolate." (Daniel 9:27)

Many teach that the "covenant" of Daniel 9 is a *peace* treaty, and there will be three and a half years of peace during the first half of the Great Tribulation. This view is completely unfounded, yet it has been repeated so many times over the years that many believe it without any Scriptural evidence.

It is *assumed* that the "covenant" of the Little Horn is a "covenant of peace." However, when we look at the original Hebrew, the word translated "confirm"[1] means to "prevail, be mighty, have strength, be great" (Theological Wordbook of the Old Testament.) So we could translate this passage:

"He shall make a strong covenant with many for one week"
(New Revised Standard Version, English Standard Version)
or
"He will strike a firm alliance with many people for the space
of a week" (New Jerusalem Bible)

This is not a covenant of peace; it is an alliance of war. It is a covenant that brings power, and strength. There is also another passage in Daniel that appears to teach that the Antichrist will establish a covenant of peace. According to a few English translations, we read that the Little Horn destroys or corrupts (*shachath*) through peace:

"And through his policy also he shall cause craft to prosper in his hand; and he shall magnify himself in his heart, <u>and by</u> <u>peace shall destroy</u> <u>many</u>: he shall also stand up against the

---
[1] גָּבַר *gabar*

Prince of princes; but he shall be broken without hand."
(Daniel 8:25, King James Version)

The word "peace" comes from a Hebrew word which means "quietness" or "prosperity[1]." Since Daniel predicted that the Antichrist begins his rise to power with "great words" (Daniel 7:11,) and after "an army is given to him" (Daniel 8:12,) the proper translation of this passage should be "prosperity," because this ruler will not be "quiet," but threatening. Consider the Darby translation of this passage:

"And through his cunning shall he cause craft to prosper in his hand; and he will magnify himself in his heart, and by prosperity will corrupt many; and he will stand up against the Prince of princes: but he shall be broken without hand." (Daniel 8:25, The Darby Bible)

The Little Horn will rise from Assyria, and it is well known that this region has a large supply of the world's oil. From this, we can extrapolate that the Little Horn will corrupt the nations of the world through *prosperity*, not peace.

Only one additional passage comes *close* to describing a time of peace during the Great Tribulation, which is: "when they shall *say* peace and safety, then sudden destruction shall come" (1 Thessalonians 5:3.) This is a prophecy of a *discussion* of peace. There is nothing in this passage that suggests peace will actually occur. Israel has been *talking* about peace for a long, long time.

The covenant of Daniel 9 is *not* a peace treaty, but it is a covenant that brings military power, and strength to the Little Horn. In a subsequent chapter, we will learn that the use of nuclear weapons against the Psalm 83 confederacy will somehow trigger a nuclear holocaust. Edom will be destroyed merely 30 minutes before fire destroys one third of the world.

---

[1] שַׁלְוָה *shalvah*

AN ISRAELI ASSAULT AGAINST GAZA

According to the prophet Isaiah, an Israeli assault against Gaza could be the first step in the war that leads to Edom's destruction. In Isaiah chapter 11, the prophet writes about the second return of Israel in verses 11-12, and then predicts this battle will occur:

> "But they shall fly upon the shoulders of the Philistines toward the west; they shall spoil them of the east together: they shall lay their hand upon Edom and Moab; and the children of Ammon shall obey them. And the LORD shall utterly destroy the tongue of the Egyptian sea; and with his mighty wind shall he shake his hand over the river, and shall smite it in the seven streams, and make *men* go over dryshod." (Isaiah 11:14-15)

Isaiah wrote that Israel would "fly upon the shoulders of the Philistines toward the west," and "spoil them of the east." In the Hebrew, they literally "fly in" or "fly among" the Philistines, or Gaza. Therefore, this is likely a prophecy of an Israeli air strike against this land. It appears that Gaza will be the starting point of this regional conflict. Of course, the Gaza Strip is populated with many Islamic militants.

The phrase "lay their hand" literally means "send[1] their hand," or "put forth their hand" as translated by the Jewish Publication Society:

> "And they shall fly down upon the shoulder of the Philistines on the west; together shall they spoil the children of the east; they shall put forth their hand upon Edom and Moab; and the children of Ammon shall obey them." (Isaiah 11:14, JPS translation)

After Israel will "fly into Gaza," and "spoil them of the east"—they will "send forth their hand" on Edom and Moab. The people of the "east" could refer to Arabs living in Syria, or even the Palestinians in Judea. Of course, there would also be an uprising in these regions.

---

[1] The word "lay" is from x;Alv.mi mishlowach, which means, "sending forth."

Throughout the Bible, the "hand" is a symbol of power and strength. Since several prophecies teach that Israel will destroy Edom by fire, this fiery destruction could be the "hand" Israel will "put forth." Isaiah continues, by prophesying that the tongue of the Egyptian sea will be destroyed at this time:

"And the LORD shall utterly destroy the tongue of the Egyptian sea; and with his mighty wind shall he shake his hand over the river, and shall smite it in the seven streams, and make men go over dryshod." (Isaiah 11:15)

The "tongue of the Egyptian Sea is the northern tip of the Red Sea, which was a port of the ancient empire of Edom. While this "tongue" has been slowly receding for hundreds of years, it has not been utterly destroyed, as Isaiah predicted. When John paraphrases the destruction of Edom in the "sixth seal," he adds: "every mountain *and island* were moved out of their places..." (Revelation 6:14.) And the prophet Jeremiah wrote that "the earth is moved at the sound of their fall" and their cry was "heard in the Red Sea" (Jeremiah 49:21). These prophecies suggest that the destruction of Edom will be so massive, the whole area will be affected, including the northern tip of the Red Sea. Obviously, this confederacy would also attack by sea.

Southwestern Jordan will only be *one* staging ground for this attack. The "Philistines" will obviously attack from Gaza; Tyre, and Gebal from Lebanon. The destruction of Edom in Jordan appears to be the final stage in a regional war. Israel will "put forth" her "hand" at this time, and fire will destroy all troops assembled in the land once called Edom.

THE LOUD SILENCE OF PSALM 83
Written July, 2014

"<A Song or Psalm of Asaph.> Keep not thou silence, O God: hold not thy peace, and be not still, O God. For, lo, thine enemies make a tumult: and they that hate thee have lifted up the head. They have taken crafty counsel against thy people, and consulted against thy hidden ones. They have said, Come, and let us cut them off from being a nation; that the name of Israel may be no more in remembrance. For they have consulted together with one consent: they are confederate against thee: The tabernacles of Edom, and the Ishmaelites; of Moab, and the Hagarenes; Gebal, and Ammon, and Amalek; the Philistines with the inhabitants of Tyre; Assur also is joined with them: they have holpen the children of Lot. Selah. Do unto them as unto the Midianites ...O my God, make them like a wheel; as the stubble before the wind. As the fire burneth a wood, and as the flame setteth the mountains on fire; So persecute them with thy tempest, and make them afraid with thy storm." (Psalm 83:1-15)

This prophecy has never been fulfilled. And take note—Edom is the first region listed in this prophecy:

"The tents of Edom, and the Ishmaelites..."

Since the Psalmist used the term "tents" in reference to Edom, this could indicate that the *people* of this region gather against Israel, not their governments. However, it could also mean something else quite profound. A tent is used by a nomad, someone who moves place to place. Therefore, Edom's inhabitants are troops that are camped there, ready for war. And, since they are gathered to attack Israel—and Edom was on Israel's eastern border—most of the Psalm 83 coalition would be gathered there, minis Philista (or Gaza) attacking from the West.

The Psalmist wrote that "Assur is joined with them." The power of the Psalm 83 coalition appears to be Assur, or Assyria.

The word transliterated "Assur" in Psalm 83 is also mistranslated "the Assyrian" in numerous Bible prophecies, which describe the Antichrist, or the "little horn" in Scripture. Even though numerous prophets describe God descending from the heavens to judge a ruler also called the "king of Seshach" (another term for Babylon) by the prophet Jeremiah (Jeremiah 25:26,) the translation "Assur" or "Assyria" is correct. This refers to a specific region of land, not one ruler.

Now, Scripture makes two seemingly contradictory claims. The Psalmist wrote that the tents of Assur are destroyed at the beginning of the Great Tribulation. Yet, at the same time, Assyria will be judged at the end of the Great Tribulation, when the Messiah returns:

"Now gather thyself in troops, O daughter of troops: he hath laid siege against us: they shall smite the judge of Israel with a rod upon the cheek. But thou, Bethlehem Ephratah, though thou be little among the thousands of Judah, yet out of thee shall he come forth unto me that is to be ruler in Israel; whose goings forth have been from of old, from everlasting. Therefore will he give them up, until the time that she which travaileth hath brought forth: then the remnant of his brethren shall return unto the children of Israel. And he shall stand and feed in the strength of the LORD, in the majesty of the name of the LORD his God; and they shall abide: for now shall he be great unto the ends of the earth. <u>And this man shall be the peace, when the Assyrian shall come into our land</u>: and when he shall tread in our palaces, then shall we raise against him seven shepherds, and eight principal men. And <u>they shall waste the land of Assyria with the sword</u>, and the land of Nimrod in the entrances thereof: thus shall he deliver us from the Assyrian, when he cometh into our land, and when he treadeth within our borders." (Micah 5:1-6)

As stated, numerous translations incorrectly render "Assyria" as "the Assyrian." Instead, it should translated "Assyria":

"And this one hath been peace, Asshur! when he doth come into our land, And when he doth tread in our palaces, We have raised against him seven shepherds, And eight anointed of man. And they have afflicted the land of Asshur with the sword, And the land of Nimrod at its openings, And he hath delivered from Asshur when he doth come into our land, And when he treadeth in our borders." (Micah 5:5-6, Young's Literal Translation)

Assyria will come into the land of Israel in the latter days, and then be judged by the Lord. In Micah's prophecy, it is clearly the region of land that is identified by the prophets, not the ethnicity of one specific ruler. Yet, take note of the striking differences in these prophecies.

1. In Psalm 83, Assur is destroyed with the coalition
2. In Micah, Assur is destroyed after the Messiah comes

1. In Psalm 83, Assur is destroyed before invading Israel
2. In Micah—and numerous prophets including Isaiah—Assur does invade Israel (verse 5)

There must be a reason for these anomalies, and the current history of this region explains how these anomalies are possible. As the Great Tribulation approaches, our understanding of these prophecies becomes clearer.

The Destruction of Edom
Begins the Judgment Day of God

In Isaiah's prophecy, and it's paraphrase in Revelation 6:17. the destruction of Edom begins the judgment day of God. And, the description of how the troops of the Psalm 83 coalition are destroyed matches Isaiah's description of Edom's destruction:

O my God, make them like a wheel; as the stubble before the wind. As the fire burneth a wood, and as the flame setteth the mountains on fire; So persecute them with thy tempest, and make them afraid with thy storm." (Psalm 83:1-15)

"Come near, ye nations, to hear; and hearken, ye people: let the earth hear, and all that is therein; the world, and all things that come forth of it. For the indignation of the LORD is upon all nations, and his fury upon all their armies: he hath utterly destroyed them, he hath delivered them to the slaughter. Their slain also shall be cast out, and their stink shall come up out of their carcases, and the mountains shall be melted with their blood. And all the host of heaven shall be dissolved, and the heavens shall be rolled together as a scroll: and all their host shall fall down, as the leaf falleth off from the vine, and as a falling fig from the fig tree. For my sword shall be bathed in heaven: behold, it shall come down upon Idumea, and upon the people of my curse, to judgment. The sword of the LORD is filled with blood, it is made fat with fatness, and with the blood of lambs and goats, with the fat of the kidneys of rams: for the LORD hath a sacrifice in Bozrah, and a great slaughter in the land of Idumea. And the unicorns shall come down with them, and the bullocks with the bulls; and their land shall be soaked with blood, and their dust made fat with fatness. For it is the day of the LORD'S vengeance, and the year of recompences for the controversy of Zion. And the streams thereof shall be turned into pitch, and the dust thereof into brimstone, and the land thereof shall become burning pitch. It shall not be quenched night nor day; the smoke thereof shall go up for ever: from generation to generation it shall lie waste; none shall pass through it for ever and ever." (Isaiah 34:1-10)

Isaiah wrote that Edom would be destroyed by fire. In the book of Revelation, the John paraphrases this prophecy, and the people of the earth cry "the great day of His wrath has come" (Revelation 6:17.) This echoes Isaiah, who writes that this prophecy would be fulfilled when " the indignation of the LORD is upon all nations." This is the beginning of the Great Tribulation.

Since the Psalmist listed the "tents of Edom" first in this coalition, this attempted invasion must cause Edom's destruction. Compare this to Jeremiah, who wrote that Israel will destroy these troops:

"Thus saith the Lord GOD; Because that Edom hath dealt against the house of Judah by taking vengeance, and hath greatly offended, and revenged himself upon them; Therefore thus saith the Lord GOD; I will also stretch out mine hand upon Edom, and will cut off man and beast from it; and I will make it desolate from Teman; and they of Dedan shall fall by the sword. And I will lay my vengeance upon Edom by the hand of my people Israel: and they shall do in Edom according to mine anger and according to my fury; and they shall know my vengeance, saith the Lord GOD." (Ezekiel 25:12-14)

Israel will destroy Edom with fire at the beginning of the Great Tribulation. This strongly suggests the use of nuclear weapons. However, we must ask ourselves: if Assur is judged in the Psalm 83 coalition at the *beginning* of the Great Tribulation, how could it invade Israel, and be judged at the end? The answer to this question lies in the two factions of Islam. While some believe that the destruction of the Psalm 83 coalition will cause *all* of Islam to be diminished, the facts modern history brings us to a different conclusion.

The "Islamic Republic of Iraq"

The "Islamic Republic of Iraq" has been formed in the regions of eastern Syria, and western Iraq—the same location as ancient Assyria. This is an extremist Sunni Muslim group, with ties to Al Qeida. According to this news report, this group wants to form a caliphate or empire in the Middle East:

"The Islamic State of Iraq and Syria (ISIS) continued its consolidation of power on the Iraq-Syria border over the weekend, but U.S. officials and experts warn that the Sunni Islamic militants may not end its quest for power even if it takes over Iraq. The group's name also translates to the Islamic State of Iraq and the Levant, a swath of land across the Middle East that includes Syria, Jordan, Lebanon and Israel - and that's exactly where the militants may be headed." (IRAQ IS NOT THE LAST STOP FOR ISIS. CBS News, June 23, 2014[1])

Except for Kuwait, the list of nations that would be part of this "caliphate" is identical to the ancient Babylonian empire, as stated in my book Rise of the Assyrian, first written in 2006:

"Historically, the modern nations that were once part of the Babylonian empire were Iraq, Syria, Jordan, Lebanon and parts of Egypt, and Israel. By process of elimination, the three nations likely to be subdued by the Antichrist are Lebanon, Syria and Jordan. Half of Israel will not be subdued, and it is unlikely that a Palestinian nation will be established during the Great Tribulation. The Little Horn will control the West Bank and Gaza, but not as independent states." (Rise of the Assyrian, third edition, page 218)

---

[1] *At the time of this publication:* http://www.cbsnews.com/news/iraq-likely-isnt-the-last-stop-for-isis/

The desire of this group to form an empire or caliphate in this region aligns with Bible prophecy. However, I believe that this group will fail, based on the prophecy of Psalm 83. The defeat of this group by Israel in Jordan would give rise to another group, who has the same ambitions. It is apparent that the current alignments against this Sunni terrorist group could explain the alliance between the "little horn" (who only subdues three kingdoms, according to Daniel (Daniel 7:14,24), and the rise of "mystery Babylon"—the capital city of a similar empire in the latter days.

The List of Nations

Of course, the Psalmist begins with the phrase "tents of," which implies that this army will be made of the individual tribes or peoples, not nations—called "kings" in Scripture. Edom, the place where this destruction will occur, is an area in western Jordan, along the Israeli border. Recently, the leader of ISIS called for 15 thousand "jihadist fighters" to assemble in Jordan, and attack Israel:

"Members of the Islamic State of Iraq and Syria are claiming on jihadist websites that the group is preparing an operation in which more than 15,000 of its militants will storm into Jordan, WND has found. The claims were made on Arabic jihadist websites in which the Islamic State of Iraq and Syria, or ISIS, is known to be active. While it was unclear whether or not the ISIS could fulfill its threat to storm Jordan, the al-Qaida-inspired group on Sunday reportedly seized control of Iraq's main border crossing with Jordan." (ISIS THREATENS TO STORM JORDAN WITH 15,000 FIGHTERS. World Net Daily, June 23, 20141)

The words of the leader of this group echo the words of the Psalmist. A call has been made for an alliance against Israel, in order to destroy it. And, the people who would heed this Sunni could easily

---

[1] *At the time of this publication:* http://www.wnd.com/2014/06/isis-threatens-to-storm-jordan-with-15000-fighters/

fulfill the people assembled in this coalition, and would exclude others.

The next group on this list are the Ishmaelites. The Ishmaelites are considered to be a descendent of all Arab peoples. However, they are also a tribe of Arabs, who dwell on the borders of Israel (currently in Jordan):

"Ishmaelites "...nomads on the borders of Palestine..." (Jewish Virtual Library)

The term "Hagarenes" could also be used for all Arab peoples, but also a tribe who dwelt in this same region. Moab, Ammon and Gebel also are areas currently in Jordan. Thus Arabs in Jordan will join in this coalition, and Edom in western Jordan is where they will be assembled, ready to invade.

Amalek can refer to the Palestinians. The Philistines (or Philista) dwelt in the modern day Gaza Strip, the area that Israel has now invaded. And of course, Assur is Assyria—the region that ISIS has now established a "caliphate" —in east Syria and Western Iraq, exactly the location of ancient Assyra.

There is one description of a certain region however, that has been often overlooked. We read

"the inhabitants of Tyre"

Now, why would this distinction be made? Why did the Psalmist not write: "the inhabitants of Moab," or "the inhabitants of Ammon?" Current history has given us a reason for this distinction. But first, it should be mentioned that Tyre is specifically identified as a region aligned with the Antichrist's latter day empire, or caliphate. It should also be noted that the modern city of Tyre has a *Shia* majority, but we are now witnessing a *Sunni* uprising.

In this distinction—Sunni vs Shia—lies the answer to the "loud silence of Psalm 83." This "silence" is a question that should have been asked, but never has been until now.

There is a reason Tyre could play a role in both a Sunni uprising now, and a Shia caliphate later. Because of the civil war in Syria, Palestinian refugees are flooding into Lebanon—and now settling in the city of Tyre:

> "The Palestine Refugees in South Lebanon live in the city of Tyre, villages around the city and towards the Israeli border and in three camps: El-Buss (1.5km south-east of the city of Tyre), Burj el-Shemali (3km east of Tyre) and Rashidieh (on the seashore 5km south of Tyre)...With the outbreak of the conflict on 12-13 July the Palestine refugee camps saw both inflows and outflows of displaced people. A survey conducted two weeks after the outbreak of hostilities estimated the population of the three camps at 25,363, with 2,920 having left the camps, and 22,443 left behind. While UNRWA has no precise data on the whereabouts of those who left, the community reports that most have gone to friends and family in the Palestinian camps in Saida. Palestinian IDPs from the Tyre area are believed to be among the 5,376 IDPs who have arrived in the Saida camps since the start of the conflict." (THE SITUATION OF PALESTINE REFUGEES IN SOUTH LEBANON. The Electronic Intifada, August 15, 2014[1])

The phrase "inhabitants of Tyre" perfectly describes these refugees. They are not from Tyre, by are "inhabitants of Tyre." Furthermore, even if this group is a *mixture* of Shia and Sunni Muslims, as Palestinians they would certainly want to help defeat Israel, and establish a Palestinian State. However, the rest of the Islamic world, the Shia, and moderate Sunni, fear this terrorist group, and are attempting to stop it. In this situation, we are witnessing "strange bedfellows" and this reveals the answer to the "loud silence" of Psalm 83.

---

[1] *At the time of this publication:* http://electronicintifada.net/content/situation-palestine-refugees-south-lebanon/2712

The "Loud Silence"

The "Loud Silence" of this Psalm is a question all theologians should have asked based on the nations *not* listed in by the Psalmist. There are many nations that were enemies of Israel, which are not listed among those in the Psalm 83 coalition. These nations are:

Egypt
Persia (Iran)
Syria

Now, these nations are geographically near Israel, and have always been enemies. Yet, the circumstances of this Sunni uprising—already "establishing" a nation in the region once called Assyria—perfectly explain why Egypt, Iran, and Syria would not join in this battle.

Let us consider Egypt. Egypt is a majority Shia. The terrorists in Gaza however, are Sunni. They are members of Al-Qieda. Egypt right now is sitting back, and letting Israel invade to wipe them out:

"Throughout the last three long years, Hamas was planning with the Brotherhood to overthrow the Egyptian regime and seize power, and the Brotherhood organization had already succeeded to "hijack" the revolution. During Morsi's and the Brotherhood rule, Egypt's lands and border crossings were opened wide to Hamas and the Palestinians, and the Brotherhood sent them food, fuel, medicine and money in huge quantities, while the Egyptians were suffering from major crises in fuel, and the disappearance of many kinds of medicine and high food prices— it was as if the Brotherhood just ruled Egypt for the benefit of Hamas... not for Egyptians. When Egyptians revolted against the Brotherhood and overthrew them, leaders Hamas went postal, filling their hearts with desires for revenge against the Egyptians, to make them pay the price for their refusal of that brotherhood terrorist group. Hamas sought with all its powers to ignite the Egyptian reality by entering large numbers of terrorists through tunnels in Sinai, as they smuggled tons of weapons, and distributed bombs across Egypt to be used later in the killing of the Egyptians. They only recently began to assist terrorists called "ISIS" to be able to settle and spread in North Sinai in preparation for declaring Sinai as an Islamic State belonging to the new caliphate, which was announced by ISIS only days ago. After this history, is it really any wonder why the Egyptians no longer have sympathy for the Palestinians of Gaza when Israel bombs Gaza, targeting leaders of Hamas and other terrorist groups that spread on the border of Egypt?" (WHY THE EGYPTIANS HAVE NO SYMPATHY FOR THE PALESTINIANS OF GAZA DURING THE ISRAELI BOMBARDMENT. Canada Free Press, July 14, 2014[1])

Egypt fears ISIS, as any other Shia nation would. In Syria, and Iraq, ISIS has been killing the Shia, and tearing down their shrines. We have also witnessed Iran publicly declaring that it would not rule out an alliance with the United States, to fight against this terrorist group:

"The largely Shia Iranian government has close links to the Shia Iraqi government that came in to power after former leader Saddam Hussein was overthrown.Both are seen as infidels by the Sunni group Isis." (IRAQ CRISIS: IRAN COULD JOIN FORCES WITH US TO HALF NEIGHBOUR'S JUHADI THREAT. The Independent, Friday July 25, 2014[2])

Of course, Syria is now in a war with ISIS, which explains why it would definitely not join in this coalition. So, every nation that you would expect to join in a coalition against Israel—that have fought against it throughout it's history—would not be part of the Psalm 83 coalition, according to the circumstances of recent history.

---

[1] *At the time of this publication:* http://canadafreepress.com/index.php/article/64560
[2] *At the time of this publication:* http://www.independent.co.uk/news/world/middle-east/iraq-crisis-iranian-president-hassan-rouhani-says-we-are-ready-to-help-9537171.html

Since these groups will gather in Jordan, we should witness Jordan fall to ISIS soon.

The Coalition of Nations, and Diminished Sunni Power in the Middle East

The destruction of a Sunni lead terrorist group by Israel would diminish the power of the Sunni in that region, and allow the Shia to take over these fallen nations. We read that the Little Horn will subdue three fallen kingdoms, "plucked up by the roots":

"I was considering the horns, when another horn appeared, a little one coming up among them; to make room for it, three of the earlier horns were plucked up by the roots. There were eyes like human eyes in this horn, and a mouth speaking arrogantly." (Daniel 7:8, New Revised Standard Version)

"And the ten horns out of this kingdom are ten kings that shall arise: and another shall rise after them; and he shall be diverse from the first, and he shall subdue three kings." (Daniel 7:24)

The Antichrist will subdue three kings, defined as "earlier horns"— a "horn" symbolizing a warring nation (because a horn is the weapon of an animal.) These three fallen kings are identified in Scripture, as Lebanon, Syria, and Jordan. If these nations are united with Iraq, this would reform the "Babylonian Empire," since this same region was once ruled by Babylon.

The dream of such an empire is shared by both Shia and Sunni. Only the man who will rule aover this caliphate in the last three and a half years of the Great Tribulation will first receive support by the nations of the world.

A Shia ruler from Iraq could achieve such an alliance, in a fight against ISIS. After all, the Antichrist is a "little horn"—a small military leader—at the time he forms this "covenant." Thus it is possible we could witness the nations of the world form an alliance with him, first *against* the Psalm 83 coalition—formed by ISIS—and then against Israel.

The timing of the rise of ISIS perfectly aligns with the interpretation of Daniel's Seventy Seven prophecy, as presented in my book "the Seventh Shmita." This method of interpretation, also embraced by the famed scientist Isaac Newton, points to the seventh "Sabbatical Year" or Shmita as the year of this "covenant" or alliance.

The same Hebrew word translated "confederacy" in Psalm 83, is translated "covenant" in Daniel 9:27, regarding the little horn. Since the term "horn" symbolizes a military ruler, this could be a military alliance, in a fight against the Sunni alliance ISIS, now called the Islamic State in Iraq and the Levant (ISIL). This alliance of the little horn could begin as a response to ISIS, yet continue against Israel in the middle of the Great Tribulation.

After the United States is destroyed in a nuclear war, the nations of the world might blame Israel for causing this catastrophe, since their use of nuclear weapons against the coalition in Edom will proceed the destruction of one third of the world by fire. This destruction will occur only thirty minutes after Israel the Psalm 83 coalition becomes dust, as the mountains are set on fire.

After this, a multinational army will support the little horn in his quest to force Israel from the Temple Mount in the middle of the Great Tribulation, according to the Word of God.

THE NUCLEAR DEVASTATION
From the Book "Rise of the Assyrian"
First written 2006

*T*he prophet Isaiah made a startling prediction of a catastrophic event that will occur during the Great Tribulation. In Isaiah chapter 24, we read:

"Behold, the LORD maketh the earth empty, and maketh it waste, and turneth it upside down, and scattereth abroad the inhabitants thereof. And it shall be, as with the people, so with the priest; as with the servant, so with his master; as with the maid, so with her mistress; as with the buyer, so with the seller; as with the lender, so with the borrower; as with the taker of usury, so with the giver of usury to him. The land shall be utterly emptied, and utterly spoiled: for the LORD hath spoken this word. The earth mourneth and fadeth away, the world languisheth and fadeth away, the haughty people of the earth do languish. The earth also is defiled under the inhabitants thereof; because they have transgressed the laws, changed the ordinance, broken the everlasting covenant. Therefore hath the curse devoured the earth, and they that dwell therein are desolate: therefore <u>the</u> <u>inhabitants of the earth are burned, and few men left</u>." (Isaiah 24:1-6)

According to this prophecy, a time will come when the inhabitants of the world will be burned, and only a few survive. If we compare Isaiah's prophecy to modern technology, it is reasonable to conclude that the prophet foresaw a nuclear holocaust.

This chapter will examine Biblical prophecies that could be fulfilled by a nuclear war. This explains the true nature of the "Great Tribulation"—and why it will be the most horrific time in human history:

"And at that time shall Michael stand up, the great prince which standeth for the children of thy people: <u>and there shall be a time of trouble, such as never was since there was a nation even to that same time</u>: and at that time thy people shall be delivered, every one that shall be found written in the book." (Daniel 12:1)

"<u>For in those days shall be affliction, such as was not from the beginning of the creation which God created unto this time, neither shall be.</u> And except that the Lord had shortened those days, no flesh should be saved: but for the elect's sake, whom he hath chosen, he hath shortened the days." (Mark 13:19-20)

No other time of affliction will compare to the Great Tribulation. Jesus explained that if it were not for the fact that this time will be "cut short," man would not survive. This time will be "cut short" by the return of Christ to the earth to rescue mankind from self-annihilation.

Revelation Chapter 8

We had previously learned that three events will occur after the "sixth seal" is removed from the "Scroll of Judgment":

(1) The judgment of Edom [Isaiah 34:4-5, Revelation 6:12-13]
(2) The sealing of 144,000 Jewish converts [Revelation 7:1-8]

(3) The Rapture of the Church [Revelation 7:9-17]

Since three events are all part of the "sixth seal," this likely means they will occur almost simultaneously. As the "sixth seal" concludes, many will hide underground, and recognize that the "great day" of God's wrath has begun (Revelation 6:17.) After the "seventh seal" is removed, the scroll will be opened in *30 minutes*:

"And when he had opened the seventh seal, there was silence in heaven about the space of half an hour." (Revelation 8:1)

The "Seventh Seal" is one "half hour of silence." This is extremely profound. Since God's heaven is timeless, this "half hour" occurs in the "heaven" of the earth's atmosphere. It is well-known that a nuclear exchange between Russia, and the United States would only take 30 minutes:

"A Topol missile launched from a silo at Plesetsk, a Russian ICBM base, could hit the United States in 30 minutes." (From a text adaptation of CNN's Special Report, "Rehearsing Doomsday.")

The "seventh seal" will last for the same amount of time as a nuclear exchange between Russia and the United States. Since Revelation chapter 8 precisely describes a nuclear war in every detail, this could be why God chose this amount of time.

Israel's use of nuclear weapons against the troops amassing in Jordan will somehow trigger this nuclear holocaust—destroying one-third of the world. This destruction could hide the fact that the rapture has occurred. In the aftermath of this nuclear exchange, many would assume that the missing Christians merely died in the devastation.

The Four Trumpets are Grouped Together

After the Scroll of Judgment is opened, seven "trumpets" are blown. In Biblical times, the "trumpet" was a ram's horn, which was used to warn of impending destruction, or announce the coming of a King. The symbol of a trumpet in Revelation could warn of either of these events, or both.

The events that correspond to the first four "trumpets" describe a nuclear holocaust with great precision. The first four trumpets are grouped together in a set, and the remaining three trumpets take place sometime later. The following passage proves this assertion. After the first four trumpets are blown, we read this statement:

"And I beheld, and heard an angel flying through the midst of heaven, saying with a loud voice, Woe, woe, woe, to the inhabiters of the earth by reason of the other voices of the trumpet of the three angels, which are yet to sound!" (Revelation 8:13)

Obviously, the first four trumpets are blown in sequence about the same time, and the remaining three trumpets occur at various times during the Great Tribulation. If a great span of time existed between each of the first four trumpets, why would this angel make this statement? Obviously, the first four "trumpets" take place one after another, and the last three sometime later.

In John's vision, specific disasters occur when each of the first four "trumpets" are blown. Every "trumpet" is a warning to those living on the earth that the coming of the King is near.

The First Trumpet

When the first ram's horn is blown, one third of the world is destroyed:

"The first angel sounded, and there followed hail and fire mingled with blood, and they were cast upon the earth: and the third part of trees was burnt up, and all green grass was burnt up." (Revelation 8:7)

In this vision, the Apostle witnesses "hail and fire"—mixed with blood— falling to the earth. This fire burns up one third of the world's trees. If we compare this prophecy to the effects of a nuclear war, we discover they are identical. First, let's consider how hail is formed:

"Hail usually forms when raindrops are blown up into the high (cold) areas of a cloud and freeze." (The Concise Columbia Encyclopedia)

Many nuclear weapons are targeted high above populated areas, to kill as many people as possible. These explosions would occur beneath cloud formations (which contain water vapor.) The tremendous blast waves from these fireballs would force water vapor rapidly into the upper regions of the atmosphere. This water vapor— forced into the colder regions of the atmosphere *more violently than at any time in history*—would form hailstones.

This hail would fall to the earth about the same time as fallout, and other burning debris. The fallout would be mixed with the blood of millions of people, who had been vaporized by the heat, and sucked into the fireball. Thus "hail mixed with fire and blood" would fall to the earth as John predicted.

The soot and smoke caused by these fires would have an impact on the entire world. It would likely cause the temperature of the entire planet to drop rapidly. This phenomenon is called "nuclear winter." While most scientists today do not believe that this temperature drop would be as drastic as previously thought, there would be a drop in temperature nevertheless. These falling temperatures would cool the earth to the point that no green grass would grow for months. Furthermore, a nuclear war would weaken the ozone layer, which would destroy crops, burn any green grass, and bring famine upon the entire world.

The Second Trumpet

After one third of the world is burned by fire, one third of all sea life will be killed:

"And the second angel sounded, and as it were a great mountain burning with fire was cast into the sea: and the third part of the sea became blood; And the third part of the creatures which were in the sea, and had life, died; and the third part of the ships were destroyed." (Revelation 8:8-9)

John had a vision of something similar to "a great mountain burning with fire." This "mountain burning with fire" caused a horrifying destruction upon the earth's oceans. A nuclear weapon detonated in the ocean could be described as a "mountain burning with fire." It is also possible that this "mountain" is symbolic of one, great nation that will be destroyed in this holocaust[1].

It is well known that shipyards, and military bases, are targeted by nuclear weapons. These weapons cause the identical devastation predicted by John. One third of all sea life would be wiped out by radioactive fallout.

The Third Trumpet

Following this devastation, we read that one-third of the earth's water supply will be poisoned:

"And the third angel sounded, and there fell a great star from heaven, burning as it were a lamp, and it fell upon the third part of the rivers, and upon the fountains of waters; And the name of this star is called Wormwood: and the third part of the waters became wormwood: and many men died of the waters, because they were made bitter." (Revelation 8:10-11)

---

[1] In Revelation 17:9 the "seven mountains" are symbolic of "seven kings [kingdoms]."

The fallout caused by a nuclear war would poison the earth's water supply, as John predicted. Drinking water free from contamination would be rare. Once again, John's prophecy precisely matches the devastation caused by a nuclear war.

As stated in a previous chapter, the fireballs produced by nuclear weapons are small replications of suns. The same nuclear fission that occurs within a star is present in an atomic blast, only on a much smaller scale.

Consider, John wrote that a "star" will poison the waters—and a nuclear blast temporarily duplicates a star. God may have given John a vision of a fireball produced by one nuclear explosion to reveal the cause of this calamity. It is well known that radioactive fallout would contaminate the water supply.

The Fourth Trumpet

The devastation that corresponds to the "fourth trumpet" of John's vision is also identical to the environmental effects of nuclear weaponry. But first, let us review the events of the first three trumpets:

1. One third of the earth is burned
2. Hail, fire and blood fall to the earth
3. One third of the oceans are poisoned
4. One third of all ships are destroyed
5. One third of the earth's drinking water is contaminated

In the next "trumpet," we read that sunlight, moonlight, and starlight will be blocked from reaching one third of the world:

"And the fourth angel sounded, and the third part of the sun was smitten, and the third part of the moon, and the third part of the stars; so as the third part of them was darkened, and the day shone not for a third part of it, and the night likewise." (Revelation 8:12)

The fires caused by a nuclear war would generate massive amounts of soot and smoke, which would rise into the atmosphere, blocking sunlight from reaching the earth's surface for several months. This fact is reported in this article from the New York Times:

"**PENTAGON AGREES THAT NUCLEAR WARFARE COULD BLOCK SUN, FREEZING EARTH.** The Pentagon today accepted as valid a theory that nuclear warfare could generate enough smoke to blot out the sun, and cause severe climate cooling." (The New York Times, March 2, 1985)

Many Scriptures predict the sun will be darkened during the Great Tribulation. In the book of Joel, we read:

"Multitudes, multitudes in the valley of decision: for the day of the LORD is near the valley of decision. The sun and the moon shall be darkened, and the stars shall withdraw their shining." (Joel 3:14-15)

The prophet Isaiah wrote:

"Behold, the day of the LORD cometh, cruel both with wrath and fierce anger, to lay the land desolate: and he shall destroy sinners out of it. For the stars and the constellations thereof shall not give their light: the sun shall be darkened in his going forth, and the moon shall not cause her light to shine. And I will punish the world for their evil, and the wicked for their iniquity; and I will cause the arrogancy of the proud to cease, and will lay low the haughtiness of the terrible." (Isaiah 13:9-11)

In the book of Matthew, Jesus taught:

"Immediately after the tribulation of those days shall the sun be darkened, and the moon shall not give her light, and the stars shall fall from heaven, and the powers of the heavens shall be shaken." (Matthew 24:29)

The world will come close to annihilation during the Great Tribulation. The first four trumpets of John's vision flawlessly describe nuclear devastation. Is it merely coincidence that John described the effects of nuclear weapons in sequence? God is warning the world of the greatest disaster ever to fall upon mankind.

How the Nuclear War Might Occur

There is a "domino" theory, which asserts that if nuclear weapons are used—even on a small scale—this could trigger a nuclear disaster. The use of nuclear weapons on the battlefield could put the superpowers on alert, leading to an accidental launch. Many experts in foreign policy believe that a war in the Middle East could trigger such an accident. Besides this fact, Russia is extremely unstable. Terrorists could strike at poorly guarded nuclear facilities, or the government itself could become unstable during a crisis.

The nuclear weapons of both Russia and the United States can be re-targeted in seven minutes. In 1995, a simple mistake almost caused an accidental launch of the Russian nuclear arsenal. A Swedish rocket veered off course, and for a brief period of time, the Russian military thought this missile was launched by the United States:

"The danger is not only an intentional nuclear war but also an accidental one. The last "known" close call came in November 1995 when the monitors of the Russian Strategic Rocket Force at the Olenegorsk early warning radar site registered the launch of a U.S.-Norwegian research missile probe of the upper atmosphere. To the Russians the missile's trajectory looked like a US Trident that carries multiple nuclear warheads. This set off the alarms of the Russian nuclear weapons command with notification reaching President Boris Yeltsin, who reportedly activated his "nuclear keys" for the first time in his tenure. The fate of the United States--and perhaps the world--hung on the decision of Yeltsin, just as it did on Nikita Khrushchev and John F. Kennedy during those faithful days in October 1962." (The Humanist, March 2000 v60 i2 p9)

The Bible is clear—fire will fall at the beginning of the Great Tribulation. The nations which currently have the arsenal capable of destroying one third of the world are Russia and the United States. Unless the balance of the world's superpowers shift quickly, and other nations greatly increase their arsenals, we can expect a showdown between Russia and the United States at any time.

Recent Events

There are several events that could strain relations between Russia and the United States, leading to an accident or an intentional launch:

1. **Development of new Russian weapons**. Russia has developed a "hypersonic" missile, which can reach their targets in a briefer amount of time, and avoid all anti-missile systems.

"MOSCOW -- President Vladimir Putin warned today that the U.S.-Russian arms race is not over and called for a strengthening of his nation's nuclear and conventional forces so Moscow can better resist foreign pressure." (The Washington Times, May 10, 2006)

2. **The Conflict with Iran**. Russia is supplying Iran with the ability to refine uranium; while at the same time they publicly *appear* to be against Iran's pursuit of the bomb.

3. **Cuts in the American nuclear stockpile.** A proposed reduction in America's nuclear arms could make a first-strike by Russia more likely.

4. **Missile Defense Shield.** The expansion of NATO into former Soviet Republics has enabled the U.S. and it's allies to develop a missile defense shield near the Russian border, which is being perceived as a hostile action.

"Dmitry Medvedev, the Russian president embraced the fiery rhetoric of the Cold War threatening to target and if necessary destroy America's planned European missile defence shield once it is built. In what may be the most serious blow to US-Russia relations since President Barack Obama came to power, Mr Medvedev raised the prospect of Russia launching missile attacks on European Union member states such as Poland, Romania and Spain as well as Nato member Turkey. "I have given the armed forces the task of drawing up plans to destroy the information and command and control systems of the (US/Nato) anti-missile shield," he said... Upping the ante further, he said Russia's anxiety was so great that it would reserve the right to tear up existing nuclear arms control treaties and halt talks about new treaties. The White House immediately rebuffed Mr Medvedev, making it clear Washington would not be altering its plans in any way." (From: *DMITRY MEDVEDEV THREATENS US OVER PLANNED MISSILE DEFENCE SHIELD*. The Telegraph, November 23, 2011)

The President Decides

The power has been given to the President of the United States to decide the type of nuclear response when a crisis occurs:

"Countless studies flowed from the effort to expand nuclear options to include "smaller packages". But it was not until 1974, the year Nixon resigned, that he signed a directive setting that process in motion. Burr said the US eventually achieved an expanded range of nuclear options, in part because of the development of more accurate missiles and other weapons in years that followed." (The Scotsman, 11/25/2005)

The President has a broad range of nuclear options at his disposal. Since the Bible does not predict that the world will be *destroyed*, the President of the United States will likely choose a limited response against Russia—saving the world from annihilation.

Since the United States supports Israel, yet there is no mention of the U.S. in Biblical prophecy, America may soon be destroyed by fire. Only time will tell.

BARACK OBAMA: LAST PRESIDENT OF THE UNITED STATES
Written June, 2014

The recent release of 5 Talaban commanders demonstrates the underlying psychology that is emerging between world leaders, that explains how the superpowers could eventually "pull the trigger" and launch a limited nuclear war. The release of these terrorists appears to confirm charges filed in Egypt that President Barack Obama has terrorist ties:

> "Lawyers in Egypt have filed criminal terrorist charges with the International Criminal Courts (ICC) against Obama. The charges filed in the ICC are said to be in addition to charges filed in Egyptian courts against him and his brother, Malik Obama." (The Examiner, November 12, 2013)

Now, Obama's decision to release these terrorists could be merely incompetence—as former President Jimmy Carter asserts. Obama does not appear to be a monster. However, communist leaders might have a different view. Vladimir Putin, who was once head of the KGB, has been paranoid of the United States since the end of the cold war. Furthermore, there have been many terrorist acts committed in Russia. "Nuclear terrorism" in the form of a nuclear strike by a "closet Muslim with terrorist ties" is not out of the realm of the *Communist's imagination.*[1]

The release of the terrorists, and the ruling by the Egyptian court, is confirmation of this paranoid belief. And that is a problem. Recently, Russia has warned that the United States is planning a first strike against Russia.

> "The plan is far advanced, and the implementation of the plan is underway. As I have reported previously, US strategic doctrine was changed and the role of nuclear missiles was elevated from a retaliatory role to an offensive first strike role. US anti-ballistic missile (ABM) bases have been established in Poland on Russia's frontier, and other bases are planned. When completed Russia will be ringed with US missile bases....Anti-ballistic missiles, known as "star wars," are weapons designed to intercept and destroy ICBMs. In Washington's war doctrine, the US hits Russia with a first strike, and whatever retaliatory force Russia might have remaining is prevented from reaching the US by the shield of ABMs....the reason Washington gave for the ABM base in Poland is to protect Europe from Iranian ICBMs. Washington and every European government knows that Iran has no ICBMs and that Iran has not indicated any intent to attack Europe. No government believes Washington's reasons. Every government realizes that Washington's reasons are feeble attempts to hide the fact that it is creating the capability on the ground to win a nuclear war. The Russian government understands that the change in US war doctrine and the US ABM bases on its borders are directed at Russia and are indications that Washington plans a first strike with nuclear weapons on Russia." (Are You ready for Nuclear War? Press TV, Tuesday June 10, 2014)

---

[1] I do not claim the President Obama is a Muslim, only that communists in Russia might believe this, whcih is all that matters in this situation.

Many news analysts view this warning as merely propaganda being spread by Putin, to scare his population into submission. Yet, we must look at it through the eyes of these paranoid communists. Obama has just released 5 of the deadliest terrorists, in exchange for a traitor. Charges have been filed against the President and his brother in Egypt. And, to be fair or not, his family has Muslim connections, and many in America believe he is a Muslim.

This belief does not need to be true. All that matters—does Putin believe it? Does Putin believe Obama has terrorist ties? If he does, then Putin really believes the United States is preparing for a nuclear first strike. And, if these reports from Russia are not propaganda, Russia really is preparing for a first strike.

All of this is occurring while the United States is planning to complete the second phase of the missile defense shield in Eastern Europe, in the fall of 2014. Russia has warned that it will bomb these sites with nuclear missiles on it's completion. It has also warned of a nuclear first strike against the current "plan" for a first strike by the United States:

"Russia Warns of Nuclear Response to U.S. Global Strike Program. A senior government minister warned Wednesday that Russia could retaliate with a nuclear strike if a new U.S. military strategy threatened its security..."They may experiment with conventional weapons on strategic delivery platforms, but they must bear in mind, that if we are attacked, in certain circumstances we will of course respond with nuclear weapons," Rogozin said." (The Moscow Times, Dec. 11 2013)

The idea and philosophy that a nuclear war would not be fought because it would "destroy the planet" is refuted by Bible prophecy, and a doctrine embraced by Vatalimer Putin, called a "limited first strike," makes this possible:

"The Russian response, begun even before the conflict over Kosovo had ended, was to develop a new military doctrine. This effort was supervised by Vladimir Putin, then-secretary of

Russia's Security Council, a body similar to the National Security Council in the United States. By the time the doctrine was adopted in the spring of 2000, it was Putin who signed it in his new capacity as president. "The doctrine introduced the notion of de-escalation—a strategy envisioning the threat of a limited nuclear strike that would force an opponent to accept a return to the status quo ante. Such a threat is envisioned as deterring the United States and its allies from involvement in conflicts in which Russia has an important stake, and in this sense is essentially defensive. Yet, to be effective, such a threat also must be credible. To that end, all large-scale military exercises that Russia conducted beginning in 2000 featured simulations of limited nuclear strikes." (The Bulleten of Atomic Scientists, March 13, 2014)

Putin's doctrine of a limited first strike, combined with paranoia of Obama's terrorist ties, explains how an attack against Israel could trigger a nuclear war. Furthermore, the completion of the nuclear defense shield makes it appear to Russia that President Obama is ready for a first strike. Eastern Europe and Russia is now preparing for a nuclear war. Analysts say that this is grandstanding, Soviet propaganda. Yet, reports exist that, even if not true, reveal that a communist fear could cause a horrible reality. And the release of these terrorists by Obama further confirm these fears.

Unlike many teachers of Bible prophecy, I believe that the battles of Gog and Magog in the books of Ezekiel and Revelation are the same. It is the Psalm 83 war, leading to the destruction of Edom, that somehow causes a nuclear war between the superpowers. The timeline of these events is explained in my book Rise of the Assyrian. The use of several nuclear weapons by Israel in self-defense will be followed by the destruction of one third of the world with fire. The destruction of Edom—quoted by John in the book of Revelation—precedes the this nuclear destruction by thirty minutes. (www.bibleprophecyunsealed.com).

Furthermore, the completion of phase II of the missile defense shield in Europe fits the timeline of Daniel's "Seventy Sevens," explained in my book the "Seventh Shmita." The Seventy Sevens prophecy asserts that the Great Tribulation will begin seven Sabbatical years after Jews return to restore Jerusalem, and the Temple Mount.

Whether Obama is aligned with terrorists or not, sufficient evidence exists that the leaders of Russia might believe this, and would use nuclear weapons in a "first strike self-defense."

It does not matter if the lapdogs in the U.S. media believe Obama is aligned with terrorists, or if Liberals or Conservatives believe this. All that matters...does Vladimir Vladimirovich Putin?

And, if he does, and the missile defense shield is about to be completed—or is completed—several nuclear missiles exploded in south-Western Jordan could cause a nuclear war between the United States and Russia, especially if the superpowers are on "hair-trigger alert." If Putin does believe Obama is aligned with terrorists, he could also believe Obama would use our nuclear arsenal against his country. Putin could believe that current talk of a reduction in nuclear weapons is a ploy—until the missile defense shield is complete.

If this does occur during the Seventh Shmita after Israel returns to the Old City of Jerusalem, Barack Obama will be the last President of the United States—because this Sabbatical year (5775) begins the fall of *this year*.

CONCLUSIONS

I have compared two chapters of a book written almost ten years ago with two chapters outlining events that have occurred recently to demonstrate how a correct view of Bible prophecy can equip a Christian to understand the times. It is not because I am a genius, but because I value the Word of God over the opinions of men. Many Christians have stopped trying to study Bible prophecy because they have the wrong foundational beliefs about this issue. Theology written over two hundred years ago have shaded their view; theology preached over and over again from the pulpit, but really has no Biblical merit.

As the time of the Lord's appearing approaches, the events of the Great Tribulation become clearer. It is certain that the present occupants of the Middle East are major players in end time events, not a ruler from Europe, America, or anywhere else. It is clear that the Antichrist will rise from Assur, the same region now controlled by ISIS.

However, since Assur or Assyria is destroyed with the Psalm 83 coalition, this ruler from Assur must rise after this coalition is judged. This explains how he will gain the military support needed against Israel, in a post apocalyptic world. A fight against a Sunni terrorist group might be the catalyst a Shia leader would need to gain their trust, and approval. We will soon witness if this is the truth.

The Seventh Shmita:
Countdown to the Second Coming

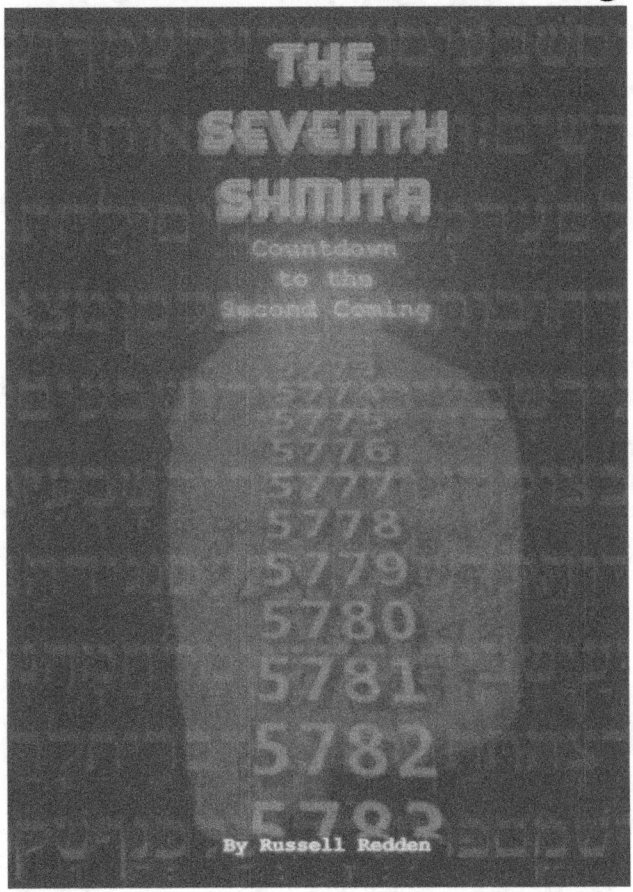

Just Released!

The Bible teaches the mystery of Daniel's prophecies are "sealed till the time of the end." As that time approaches, the mystery of Daniel's "Seventy Sevens" has been revealed. Regarded by scholars as the most difficult prophecy in the Bible to interpret, this new book reveals that Daniel's "Seventy Sevens" prophecy accurately predicted the time of Christ's birth, and also points to the next Jewish Sabbatical year (Sept. 2014-2015) as the year the Great Tribulation will begin. No one knows the day or the hour, but Daniel's prophecy does point to once specific year. This book is not based on mathematical calculations, or dispensational theories. It is based on the method of counting years given by God in the Law of Moses.

The Seventh Shmita is
Available on Amazon and Kindle

Learn the truth about Bible Prophecy

Rise of the Assyrian: The Antichrist, the Beast, and the Revived Babylonian Empire

Readers Write:

"builds a very biblical, literal, and logical interpretation of Bible prophecy"—Robert

"Significant breakthroughs in understanding some key points in prophetic scripture - much more intellectually honest than most."—Mike

This book is a comprehensive analysis of Biblical prophecy, in light of Scriptures ignored by many teachers of Eschatology today. Isaiah, Jeremiah, Ezekiel, and numerous Old Testament prophets wrote that the Messiah would defeat a wicked king in the latter days from the lands once known as Assyria or Babylon—modern day Iraq. This book presents Biblical evidence that the Antichrist will rise from this land, and temporarily establish a new "Islamic empire" in the Middle East. This empire will rise after the nations of the world force Israel from half of Jerusalem and Judea (the West Bank,) according to Bible prophecy. Learn how the predicted outcome of the Israeli/Palestinian dispute of the holy land perfectly reflects unique events of modern history, including the rise of radical Islam. Third edition.

Rise of the Assyrian is Available on Amazon and Kindle